FACEBOOK

ABDO
Publishing Company

TECHNOLOGY PIONEERS

FACEBOOK

THE COMPANY AND ITS FOUNDERS

by Ashley Rae Harris

Content Consultant
Anthony J. Rotolo
Professor of Practice,
Syracuse University iSchool

CREDITS

Published by ABDO Publishing Company, PO Box 398166, Minneapolis, MN 55439. Copyright © 2013 by Abdo Consulting Group, Inc. International copyrights reserved in all countries. No part of this book may be reproduced in any form without written permission from the publisher. The Essential Library™ is a trademark and logo of ABDO Publishing Company.

Printed in the United States of America,
North Mankato, Minnesota
062012
092012

 THIS BOOK CONTAINS AT LEAST 10% RECYCLED MATERIALS.

Editor: Megan Anderson
Series Designer: Emily Love

Library of Congress Cataloging-in-Publication Data
Harris, Ashley Rae.
  Facebook : the company and its founders / by Ashley Rae Harris.
    p. cm. -- (Technology pioneers)
  ISBN 978-1-61783-332-8
 1. Facebook (Firm)--Juvenile literature. 2. Facebook (Electronic resource)--Juvenile literature. 3. Online social networks--Juvenile literature. 4. Internet industry--United States--Juvenile literature. I. Title.
  HM743.F33H37 2013
  338.4'70046780973--dc23
                            2012005978

TABLE OF CONTENTS

Mark Zuckerberg was a sophomore at Harvard University when he launched Thefacebook.

$10 MILLION?
NO THANKS.

It was a typical summer day in June 2004 as Mark Zuckerberg and his friend Sam Lessin walked around New York City. Dressed in a T-shirt and Adidas sport sandals, the slightly shaggy-haired Zuckerberg looked the part of an American college student. He was, in fact, a sophomore at Harvard University studying computer science. Aside from his casual appearance and the student ID in his wallet, however, he was anything but average. He was about to turn down a $10 million investment offer for the little Web site he had started in his dorm room, Thefacebook.

Zuckerberg had launched Thefacebook on the Internet on February 4, 2004, just four months earlier. He had the help of his friends Eduardo Saverin, Chris Hughes, and Dustin Moskovitz. It seemed like a simple enough concept at first. The Web site was little more than an online database where Harvard students could upload photos and basic information about themselves that could be viewed by all their classmates. It had taken its name from the printed book the Harvard administration distributed to each student at the beginning of the year. This book contained pictures and contact information for the students living in each dormitory.

ADIDAS SPORT SANDALS

Mark Zuckerberg wore his telltale Adidas sport sandals very often, even to trek across Harvard's campus in the dead of winter. They became such a recognizable part of the Facebook Chief Executive Officer's (CEO) daily attire that they are worn by the manufactured, unofficial Mark Zuckerberg action figure. The figure has curly hair, freckles, wears a hoodie, and holds a "Like" sign.

POKING

"Poking" was like poking a friend in real life, except digitally. It was even more fun in the strange public/private world of Thefacebook. Some who have studied Facebook have speculated that the poking feature ended up being so popular in the company's early days because its meaning was vague. Because no one knew what it meant, or because it could mean multiple things, users were able to give it any emotional meaning they wanted.

NOT JUST A PICTURE BOOK

But what seemed simple—just a digital version of the age-old printed book—spread like wildfire across the campus within days of being posted to the Web. Within just four days of being launched, 650 students had already registered on Thefacebook. By the end of the month that number had increased to 10,000 users. Harvard students could not get enough of it.

They were logging in daily, filling out profiles about themselves with information such as their favorite bands and television shows or the political parties they supported. They were clicking on the profiles of their friends and classmates, checking to see who identified as single, who claimed to be "in a relationship," or who was just "looking for fun." They were posting inside jokes to each other's digital "walls." Many students took advantage of the

When it launched in February 2004, Thefacebook was available only to people with a harvard.edu e-mail address.

"poking" feature, which was like a digital nudge, a way to wave hello on Thefacebook.

Unlike the printed facebooks, users could create ideal images of themselves. They could select any photo they wanted to upload, often choosing images that made them look as attractive as possible. The rules were a little different on Thefacebook than in real life. It added a new dimension to campus and social life for students. On Thefacebook, the regular kids who ate lunch on the grass before biology class became glossy—"the young superstars of tomorrow, as envisioned by themselves."[1] All they needed was a valid Harvard e-mail address to participate. Judging by the reaction at Harvard, it seemed Thefacebook was exactly what people had been waiting for.

Zuckerberg and his business partner pals knew they had to ramp up and make Thefacebook available to other schools. Within less than a month, Thefacebook had launched at other Ivy League schools, long-standing colleges and universities with high academic achievement and social prestige, including Columbia, Stanford, and Yale. Several others followed shortly thereafter. Zuckerberg and Saverin each put $1,000 into Thefacebook, which they used toward five servers. Soon the two found they needed to invest another $20,000 just to keep the servers active and support the site's growth.

Thefacebook was tapping into social networking in a new way. College students all over the country were desperate to get on Thefacebook. Once Thefacebook arrived on a college's campus, it caught on quickly, which piqued the interest of investors. By May, Thefacebook had more than 100,000 users at 34 schools.

Pretty soon, Zuckerberg's school friends introduced him to businesspeople who might help him take his company to the next level. Lessin was one such friend. His father was an investor.

Lessin knew many venture capitalists and executives looking for the next great technology start-up. He and Zuckerberg headed to New York for a round of meetings with more experienced investors.

In the previous year, investors had already sunk tens of millions of dollars in other social networking sites such as SixDegrees.com, Friendster, LinkedIn, Spoke, and Tribe. They wanted a piece of Thefacebook while it was still young. One investor was so eager to buy into Thefacebook before it got big that he was willing to gamble $10 million.

It is hard to imagine any 20-year-old who could say no to that kind of money. But if the investor had

SAM LESSIN AND DROP.IO

Sam Lessin was not interested in Thefacebook just because he was a pal of Zuckerberg's. He also was a computer programmer who shared Zuckerberg's entrepreneurial spirit. A Harvard graduate, he worked as a consultant for Bain & Company before founding his own start-up in 2007 called Drop.io. Drop.io allowed users to easily drop many types of digital files into an online storage system that could be readily accessed over the Internet from any computer. Users no longer had to save files to discs or USB drives. Drop.io was voted one of the 50 Best Websites 2009 by *Time* Magazine.

Drop.io created one of the first Facebook applications that worked with the site as an online file sharing service. The company and its technology were eventually purchased by Facebook in 2010. As part of this deal struck between the two companies, Lessin went to work for Facebook. The service was shut down in December 2010 and is no longer available to users, though they were given a grace period to download and retrieve any files or data they had saved to the site.

LINKEDIN

The Web site LinkedIn was specifically designed as a tool to be used to keep track of business contacts. Users' profiles look like digital résumés. Photos are optional on LinkedIn and users generally opt for small headshots. The company continues to grow with different organizations starting "groups" and industry-specific discussion boards.

a hunch Thefacebook was going to change the world, Zuckerberg had an even greater sense of its potential. He knew his company was worth several times that offer. Thefacebook was about to become the largest, most expansive social networking site and Zuckerberg the youngest self-made billionaire in the history of the world. +

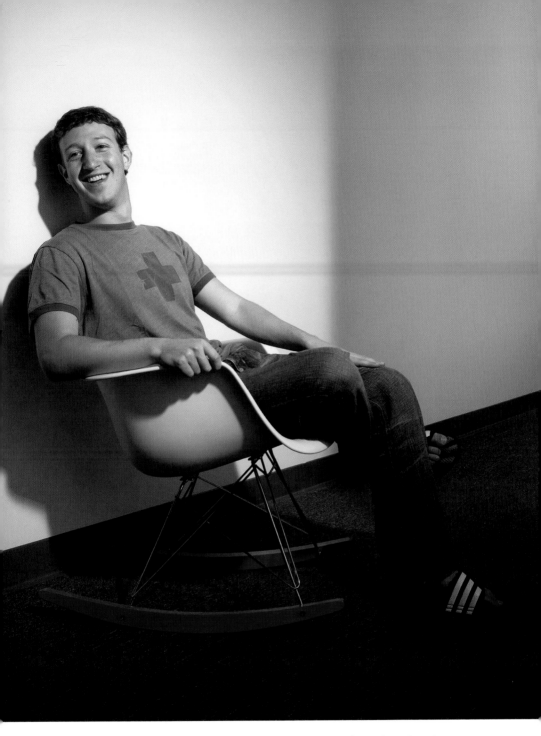

Zuckerberg was ranked fourteenth on the *Forbes* 400: The Richest People in America list in March 2012.

Zuckerberg showed exceptional computer skills at an early age.

TECH GENIUS IN THE MAKING

Mark Zuckerberg was born May 14, 1984, in Dobbs Ferry, New York. His father, Edward, was a dentist, and his mother, Karen, was a psychiatrist. Mark developed an interest in computers at a young age, and growing up there were plenty of gadgets to play with around the house. When he was 12, Mark created a computerized communication system for his dad's dentist office, which was attached to the Zuckerberg family home. It was a software program that connected the computers on the property so they could send messages to one another. With the system, called ZuckNet, the receptionist in the office could alert Dr. Zuckerberg through instant message that one of his patients had arrived. Mark's computer skills were so advanced that even his childhood computer tutor admitted, "Sometimes it was tough to stay ahead of him."[1] Mark and his three sisters also used ZuckNet to send each other messages throughout the house.

Later, while a high school student at Phillips Exeter Academy in Exeter, New Hampshire, Mark and his friend Adam D'Angelo built a software program called Synapse. Synapse worked like the music application Pandora. It collected an inventory of people's music playlists and could determine patterns of what they liked to listen to. Though Mark and D'Angelo had created Synapse for a school project, it caught the attention of the corporate world. A few big companies, including AOL Inc. and Microsoft, wanted to buy the program and hire Mark to come work for them. He declined

PANDORA

With 100 million users as of July 2011, Pandora Radio is the most widely used personalized live music-streaming source. Pandora was founded in 2000. Similar to Zuckerberg's Synapse technology, Pandora tracks music lovers' preferences based on several attributes and asks users to rate songs in order to feed them new music. Users can access Pandora for free with advertisements between songs or pay to listen without ads.

the first of many opportunities to make money off his computer genius. In the fall of 2002, he enrolled at Harvard University in Cambridge, Massachusetts.

At Harvard, Mark made a close group of friends almost immediately upon arrival, including Chris Hughes and Dustin Moskovitz. Chris and Dustin were Mark's roommates in Suite H33 in Kirkland House.

MOSKOVITZ AND HUGHES

Chris Hughes was born November 26, 1983, in Hickory, North Carolina. Chris felt out of place in his hometown and began applying to boarding schools without his parents' knowledge. With the help of a "very generous financial-aid package,"[2] Chris attended Phillips Academy preparatory school in Andover, Massachusetts. After graduating, he

Zuckerberg, Hughes, and Moskovitz were roommates in Kirkland House, one of 12 undergraduate houses at Harvard University.

attended Harvard University on a scholarship, where he studied history and literature.

Dustin Moskovitz was born May 22, 1984, in Gainesville, Florida. He is eight days younger

GEEKS AND POPULAR CULTURE

The word *geek* was originally used as an insulting remark against someone with inadequate social skills. But the word has lost much of its negative meaning and is particularly used to describe "an enthusiast or expert especially in a technological field or activity."[3]

Geek culture has also become more popular, with television shows such as *The Big Bang Theory* and "geek chic" fashion. Geek chic means wearing thick-framed glasses, cardigans, and T-shirts with technical in-jokes. Celebrities such as Justin Timberlake and David Beckham have embraced geek chic fashion.

A similar word, *nerd*, is still considered to have a negative meaning and defined as "an unstylish, unattractive, or socially inept person."[4] It was first used in the 1950 Dr. Seuss book, *If I Ran the Zoo*, to describe an angry looking old man. The 1984 movie *Revenge of the Nerds* depicts nerds as intelligent but weak, while geeks are associated with wealthy Silicon Valley innovators such as Bill Gates. Ben Nugent, author of *American Nerd: The Story of My People*, told CNN in 2010: "And so ["geek" has] come to mean something more like an empowered nerd. A nerd who is defined by his knowledge of a certain subject."[5]

than Zuckerberg. Dustin grew up in Ocala, Florida, and attended Vanguard High School. After graduating, Dustin enrolled at Harvard University, where he studied economics.

COLLEGE FOR COMPUTER GEEKS

Similar to many college students, the boys kept their first home-away-from-home in disarray with soda cans littering the floor and various books and electronics strewn about. Hughes and Moskovitz helped Zuckerberg with many of his projects. Zuckerberg launched into these computer projects with at least as much interest as he took to his studies. He was perceived as a bit geeky. Zuckerberg was small of stature, had a tendency to be quiet or moody, and he was an "intense introvert."[6]

Still, Zuckerberg received attention for Synapse and other projects, which made him somewhat popular at school. Plus, he was good at almost everything he set out to do, including subjects such as math, astronomy, physics, and classical languages. He was so smart, dry, and matter-of-fact, it was almost as if he had a computer operating in his head instead of a human brain.

One software program Zuckerberg created at Harvard was called CourseMatch. It allowed students to see which courses their classmates were signed up for. It turned out that students often based scheduling decisions on the courses their friends were taking. It was a hit around campus. Later, he would create a basic version of CourseMatch for Thefacebook. He also created something called Six Degrees of Harry Lewis, a digital graph that showed how different people on campus were connected to one of Zuckerberg's favorite professors. It was based off of the concept that everyone is connected within six degrees of one another.

SIX DEGREES OF SEPARATION

The concept that people in the world are separated from each other by no more than six introductions is the theory of the Six Degrees of Separation. This theory was the basis for the Web site SixDegrees.com. Launched by creator Andrew Weinreich in 1997, SixDegrees.com is considered to be the first successful social networking site. It allowed users to create profiles, send messages, and compile friend lists. SixDegrees.com lacked photos, and users said there was little to do after accepting friend requests. The site had 3.5 million users by 1999 and was sold to YouthStream Media Networks for $125 million in 2000. But the site closed in 2000 after failing to become a sustainable business, just as people were starting to find their way around the Internet.

FACEMASH

Though usually well liked by the students, not all of Zuckerberg's projects went over smoothly. He launched a Web site called Facemash in the middle of his sophomore year. Facemash was the brainchild of Zuckerberg and another suitemate, Billy Olson. Zuckerberg figured out a way to obtain photos of Harvard students by hacking into the school computer system. He logged in with a friend's password and downloaded the digital versions of the facebooks for various houses, or on-campus residences. Once he had the images, he developed a software program where two students' pictures would pop up on the site side-by-side. Users could click on which one was "hotter" than the other. With each click, the person deemed more attractive would move on to the next level.

Zuckerberg sometimes liked to work on a project non-stop for hours at a time until it was finished. Facemash took Zuckerberg and his pals eight hours until it was ready to launch at 4 a.m. on November 2, 2003. As soon as it hit the Web, students went bonkers. The site had 450 hits by 10:30 p.m. the following night, and students had voted on 22,000 photo pairings. The site had gone viral.

As the *Harvard Crimson* school newspaper put it:

> *A peculiarly-squinting senior and that hottie from your Medieval manuscripts section—click! Your blockmate and the kid who always glared at you in Annenberg—click! Your two best friends' respective significant others—pause . . . click, click, click! . . . We Harvard students could indulge our fondness for judging those around us on superficial criteria without ever having to face any of the judged in person.[7]*

However, it did not take long before the school administration demanded Facemash be taken down. Some groups on campus found the Web site racist and sexist, and Zuckerberg's methods for obtaining the photos were not entirely legal. After meeting with the disciplinary board, Zuckerberg was put on probation and ordered to visit with a school counselor. This was one of many episodes in which Zuckerberg's tendency to thumb his nose at rules got him into trouble.

AN EVEN BIGGER IDEA

As Zuckerberg saw the effect that CourseMatch and Facemash had on campus, he began formulating an even bigger idea—something that would really get his fellow classmates excited. Using little projects almost as tests to see what worked and what did not in the online space, Zuckerberg was beginning to create what was to become Thefacebook.

The idea behind Thefacebook was that people care—perhaps more than anything else—about the other people around them. This is especially true on a college

ZUCKERBERG, THE SLOB

While Zuckerberg has always been messy, some might say his upbringing is responsible. Zuckerberg's Harvard roommates recall his mother, Karen, apologizing when she first came to visit him at the dorm and saw the condition of his room. Her excuse for her son was, "When he was growing up he had a nanny."[8]

campus, where everyone lives in close quarters to one another and attends classes, eats, and parties together. In essence, college campuses are social networks. Zuckerberg wanted to make it easier for people to experience their real-world, physical social networks in a digital, Web-based format. He thought, rightfully so, that he would be providing a service that was highly desirable on campus.

In November 2003, Zuckerberg accepted work programming a Web site called the HarvardConnection, later named ConnectU. HarvardConnection was meant to be a dating and nightlife social networking site, aimed at Harvard students. It was started by Divya Narendra and twins Cameron and Tyler Winklevoss. Zuckerberg never signed an official agreement to help them build their site, but he verbally agreed to work for them

SIDE PROJECTS

HarvardConnection was not the only side project in which Zuckerberg was involved. Among other projects, he helped the Association of Harvard Black Women set up their Web site. It was also a way to make amends with the group. The Association of Harvard Black Women, along with the group Fuerza Latina, had previously made complaints that Facemash was sexist and racist. The side projects also helped Zuckerberg observe how people were connected in social groups at Harvard while he developed Thefacebook. "I had this hobby of just building these little projects," Zuckerberg said later. "I had like twelve projects that year. Of course I wasn't fully committed to any of them."[9]

and exchanged several e-mails about the project. His involvement with the HarvardConnection would come back to haunt him. But for now, Zuckerberg was on his way to launching what would be the biggest Internet sensation ever to hit Harvard and, eventually, the world. +

Zuckerberg and Hughes's project would rapidly become popular on Harvard's campus.

Brazilian-born Saverin helped fund Zuckerberg's idea for Thefacebook.

THINKING BUSINESS

Zuckerberg kept a white board in his room at Harvard that was covered in graphs, pie charts, sketches, and notes written in his famously tiny and meticulous script. The white board was probably a symbol of a supreme computer geek to most of his fellow students. Little did they know it contained his mental blueprint of what would become Thefacebook. Before he launched the site, Zuckerberg spoke with his friend Eduardo Saverin.

Eduardo was born March 13, 1982, in Sao Paulo, Brazil. His father, Roberto, was a wealthy Brazilian industrialist. Due to his family's wealth, Eduardo's name was placed on a list by gangs that specialized in kidnapping for ransom. Roberto and Sandra Saverin decided to move their family to Miami, Florida, in 1993. Eduardo attended Gulliver Preparatory School in Miami before attending Harvard for economics.

Zuckerberg and Eduardo worked out a business plan in which they would each invest $1,000 in Thefacebook. Initially, Zuckerberg owned two-thirds of the company, while Eduardo owned one-third. Eduardo's percentage dropped to 30 percent when Moskovitz entered the deal. To develop and grow the site, Zuckerberg would run the technical side and operations. Eduardo would be in charge of finding advertisers and bringing money into the business.

The social networking site MySpace was Thefacebook's early competition.

A BETTER SOCIAL NETWORK

Thefacebook launched at Harvard on February 4, 2004. It was not the first social networking site to hit the Internet, or even the first to get 1 million people to use it. Sites including MySpace and Friendster had already attracted millions of users by the time Zuckerberg launched Thefacebook. Thefacebook worked similarly to these sites but with some important distinctions.

Designed partly as a dating Web site where friends of friends could meet, Friendster launched in 2003. The site targeted people in their early-to-mid twenties. It was so popular the servers could not support the amount of activity the site was generating. The site would slow down or simply stop entirely, frustrating users. Server overload was one of the major problems that eventually killed the site.

MySpace launched in 2003 as a competitor of Friendster and in fact grew by attracting users that Friendster alienated. Anyone could join and use the site to communicate however they wanted, and it was a major hit immediately. It was one of the first sites that allowed kids as young as 16 to join, making it attractive to a younger audience. Some users went by fake names on their MySpace accounts, and the site encouraged users to be whoever and use the

GOING LIVE

When Thefacebook went live on February 4, 2004, its home page read:

"Thefacebook is an online directory that connects people through social networks at colleges. We have opened up Thefacebook for popular consumption at Harvard University. You can use Thefacebook to: Search for people at your school; Find out who are in your classes; Look up your friends' friends; See a visualization of your social network."[1]

Using a drop-down menu, Thefacebook users could indicate which courses they were taking, their relationship statuses, political affiliations, favorite books, and favorite quotes.

Moskovitz, *left*, helped Zuckerberg with the programming behind Thefacebook.

service however they wanted. Friendster had a policy against bands creating profiles. Bands joined MySpace instead, which became a popular place for them to interact with their fans.

With Thefacebook, Zuckerberg made no assumptions about why users would want to follow and connect with each other online. He based

Thefacebook on the expectation that people simply would want to connect for no other reason than to be connected. In Zuckerberg's reasoning, people wanted to connect with real people they knew in their offline life. He did not view Thefacebook as an alternative reality or a place where users could take on a new identity. The site was an online extension of one's real life. Friendster had imposter accounts called Fakesters, and MySpace allowed users to create profiles with different aliases. When signing up for Thefacebook, however, users agreed to Terms of Service that included using their real names and not providing false personal information.

CONNECTION IS THE KEY TO SUCCESS

After the launch, Zuckerberg's roommates Moskovitz and Hughes

THE HARVARD CRIMSON

Much of Thefacebook's early media coverage was by the *Harvard Crimson*, the college newspaper run by Harvard undergraduate students. The *Crimson* is the only daily paper in Cambridge, Massachusetts, and the only college newspaper that owns its own printing presses in the United States. Harvard junior Amelia Lester wrote about Thefacebook in the *Crimson* two days after it launched: "While Thefacebook.com isn't explicitly about bringing people together in romantic unions, there are plenty of other primal instincts evident at work here: an element of wanting to belong, a dash of vanity and more than a little voyeurism."[2]

joined Thefacebook staff. Though Moskovitz previously had limited computer skills, he helped Zuckerberg run the site. In exchange, he owned 5 percent of Thefacebook. Hughes's role dealt less with the inner workings of Thefacebook and more with its public face. Zuckerberg was not much of a talker. When he did speak, he tended to avoid eye contact. As one former friend noted, "His typical way to listen is to stare at you blankly, impassively."[3] Zuckerberg hired Hughes to help him manage publicity and speak on behalf of the company.

Thefacebook grew quickly as students started connecting with one another at Harvard University. After three weeks, Thefacebook.com had 6,000 users. Meanwhile, Zuckerberg used his college connections to support its growth.

THE COLLEGE GOLD MINE

Perhaps the biggest difference between Thefacebook and other social networking sites was that it was exclusive. In the first weeks, only Harvard students had access to the site. Moskovitz helped Zuckerberg open Thefacebook slowly, one school at a time. Thefacebook opened to Columbia on February 25, Stanford on February 26, and Yale on February 29.

Unlike MySpace, which had 1 million users from all walks of life by February 2004, Thefacebook had 10,000 users within its first month who were all Ivy League students.

Zuckerberg and Moskovitz's decision to open only to the most elite schools in the United States worked well for a few reasons. First, they created an image for Thefacebook that represented college life and exclusivity. The site's first users were among the smartest and wealthiest young people in the country. Zuckerberg assumed students at other schools would be

MYSPACE

Founded in 2003, MySpace was Thefacebook's number one competitor. MySpace remained the number one social networking site until 2008. MySpace took a different approach to profile pages, allowing users to customize their profiles using hypertext markup language (HTML).

A sort of self-segregation took place among users choosing between Thefacebook and MySpace. Danah Boyd, a research assistant professor in Media, Culture, and Communication at New York University, says that is connected to how the two sites spread and their perception. Thefacebook started out at Ivy League schools, while MySpace started out in Los Angeles, California, and spread to teenagers through the indie rock and hip-hop music scene. Many users considered Thefacebook to be more clean-cut compared to the more alternative MySpace.

MySpace memberships, traffic to the site, and revenue from advertising have since declined significantly. In 2005, it was sold for $580 million to News Corporation, one of the world's largest multimedia organizations and owner of 20th Century Fox. In June 2011, Specific Media, an interactive media company, and musician/actor Justin Timberlake purchased MySpace for $35 million, a massive decline from its peak valuation in 2007 of $12 billion.

immediately drawn to Thefacebook, almost like fighting to get into a club.

This strategy fed off the competitive personalities of many of Zuckerberg's Harvard classmates. Students were aware of their status and knew how important having the right connections were to getting ahead. To make it in the Ivy League culture, joining Thefacebook was more of a necessity than a choice. Many members gathered as many friends as possible as if it really were a popularity contest.

Opening Thefacebook to one school at a time also helped control its growth. As Zuckerberg said, "we kind of intentionally slowed it down at the beginning. We literally rolled it out school by school."[4] Thefacebook did not use the Friendster model of opening the site up to the whole world and scrambling to come up with the server support. Instead, the team sketched out a plan for where the site was going to open and when. The company also could predict how many users it could expect at each school based on the site's performance at other schools. That helped the team plan how many servers it would need to pay for and create accurate financial projections.

While Moskovitz and Zuckerberg focused on growing Thefacebook, Saverin put the official legal documents in place. In April 2004, he incorporated Thefacebook as a limited liability company in Florida. Saverin, Zuckerberg, and Moskovitz were the company's official partners. Saverin also began partnering with advertisers to bring in money to support the cost of running the site.

Zuckerberg realized early on that students did not socialize with only the people at their schools but also with students at surrounding schools. To increase the critical mass when Thefacebook opened at a new school, the site also opened to nearby schools. For example, when Thefacebook opened to students at Baylor University in Waco, Texas, it also opened to the University of Texas at Arlington, Southwestern University, and

FRIENDSTER

Friendster is said to be the original inspiration for many social networking sites, including MySpace and Thefacebook. After its success in the early 2000s, Friendster became largely obsolete in the United States. It managed to secure a significant user base in Southeast Asia until 2011, when it became a social gaming site. As of 2010, founder Jonathan Abrams continues to pursue entrepreneurial ventures in Silicon Valley.

Texas A&M. It was a highly targeted approach to growing the network.

While Thefacebook certainly benefited from good timing, smart decisions about how and where to grow the business at this early stage kept the company fairly stable. The strong foundation Thefacebook team created came in handy when the company hit the big time—and faced big obstacles—on the West Coast. +

[thefacebook]

home   search   global   social net   invite   faq   logout

[My Friends]

[export]

[global]

Export contact informa
in Outlook and other

[invite]

Find friends at other schools.

iends to join thefacebook.

[Other Schools]   [GWU]   [All]

riends

ter: [Recently Updated Profiles]

[message]   [rem

ou have 247 friends.

KIP ABER
profile updated recently

[message]   [

Harvard students flocked to Thefacebook.

Moskovitz and Zuckerberg decided to move their team to Palo Alto.

CALIFORNIA DREAMIN'

Thefacebook team entered into the social networking world with caution, testing the market each time it opened the site to a new school. But by the summer of 2004, there was no longer any doubt this was an important company with massive potential. It seemed obvious the college market was a hot spot. Investment offers rolled in, and the buzz in the technology community was getting louder.

In June 2004, Saverin secured an advertising deal with Y2M, a company that sold ads for college newspapers. Y2M's first client on Thefacebook was credit card company MasterCard. The advertising campaign went unexpectedly well, and Y2M quickly began paying for more advertising. The revenue helped pay for servers and kept Thefacebook running.

Zuckerberg wanted to go where the real action was: Silicon Valley, the home of start-up technology companies, including several social networks that had inspired Thefacebook. It was a "mythical place where all the techs used to come from."[1]

Zuckerberg and Moskovitz searched Craigslist for apartments, settling for a spot mere miles from Stanford University's campus in Palo Alto, California.

Y2M

One of Saverin's major contributions to Thefacebook was connecting the company to Y2M. As Thefacebook attempted to develop a revenue model in the financially uncharted territory of social networking, Y2M became a strategic partner and created innovative campaigns. When Thefacebook eventually built its own advertising department, Y2M employees were recruited to run it.

Adam D'Angelo agreed to come along, as did Andrew Cullom. Cullom was a programmer who had started a separate venture called Wirehog with Zuckerberg. Meanwhile, Hughes attended a summer program in France, and Saverin was interning in New York. Both of them conducted business remotely.

Zuckerberg and Saverin's approaches to the business were almost opposite. As long as the servers could be supported, Zuckerberg was not particularly focused on making money off Thefacebook. Instead, he directed all of his attention toward making sure the site's users were happy. He measured user satisfaction not only by the number of new members but also by the number of users who returned to Thefacebook regularly. As it turned out, repeat visits and prolonged time spent on Thefacebook were typical, with some users clicking through thousands of different profiles in a single session.

Zuckerberg also started strategizing his long-term vision for Thefacebook to eventually become a platform. Developers would be allowed to create applications that would exist within Thefacebook. This is similar to how different applications are created to run on the iPhone platform created by technology company Apple. An early application linked with Thefacebook was

Wirehog, a friend-to-friend file sharing program.

Zuckerberg, Moskovitz, and pals monitored all activity on Thefacebook from their new bachelor pad. The kitchen table was an informal workspace, with laptops and the constant sound of keyboards clicking. The team members dressed casually, sometimes not changing out of their pajamas before working at all hours. But they developed a productive working style, sometimes going into a trancelike state while writing computer-programming code. To avoid having their concentration disrupted, they communicated with one another with instant messages (IMs) rather than talking aloud in the same room.

When they were not busy coding and trying to run a business, Thefacebook crew still behaved like other college students. They threw parties and built a zip line from the roof into the swimming pool. Houseguests were abundant and sometimes stayed

WIREHOG

Wirehog was a file sharing program that allowed users to exchange files and videos. The program was linked to the Thefacebook starting in October 2004, part of Zuckerberg's strategy for Thefacebook to become a platform. He devoted a fair amount of his time to building it before finally realizing it lacked the simplicity and usability that had made Thefacebook popular. Wirehog was taken down in January 2006.

for weeks on end. With everyone working and living under the same roof, Thefacebook headquarters was similar to a fraternity house.

Saverin's physical distance from Thefacebook further separated him from his business partners. He was sometimes kept in the dark about daily activities or new plans. At the same time, Zuckerberg had become close to a new confidante, Sean Parker.

SEAN PARKER

Parker was something of a legend in Silicon Valley for starting Napster, a music file sharing service that made headlines in the early 2000s. Parker had more experience than anyone on Thefacebook team, even though he was not much older than any of them. From first-hand experience, Parker knew much more about business, venture capitalists, and the legal pitfalls facing technology start-ups than Zuckerberg or his partners.

Parker looked slick with designer jeans, expensive sneakers, and the right connections. In reality, he was being driven out of another company he had started, Plaxo, and was in a tough spot. It was the perfect time for him to get involved with Thefacebook.

Parker provided advice to the inexperienced Zuckerberg.

Thefacebook team members ran into Parker on the street near their apartment shortly after their arrival in California. Almost immediately, Zuckerberg and Parker began hanging out and talking business. Thefacebook was getting a lot of attention from seasoned businesspeople. It was comforting to Zuckerberg that he could go to Parker for advice. It was not long until Parker was living at Thefacebook team headquarters, sleeping on a mattress on the floor.

Zuckerberg began bringing Parker to business meetings and introducing him as president of Thefacebook. Zuckerberg was CEO, and referred to himself as "Founder, Master and Commander, Enemy of the State"[2] on Thefacebook Web site. Moskovitz took the title of "No Longer Expendable Programmer, Paid Assassin."[3]

Meanwhile, Zuckerberg and Saverin were arguing more and more about how to run the company. Saverin was still new to business dealings, and Zuckerberg felt he could rely more on Parker for his expertise. Moskovitz

PARKER AND NAPSTER

Parker has no college education, but he is known for his natural business and entrepreneurial skills. Parker began his career at age 15 as an intern at the Washington DC–based Internet start-up company Freeloaded. At 19, he founded the file sharing Web company Napster with Shawn and John Fanning.

Napster was wildly popular between 1999 and 2001, with a peak user base of 26 million people. It attracted a great deal of media attention when famous music groups such as Metallica sued the company for helping millions of users share copyrighted songs without paying for them. Though in some cases Napster helped promote the music of independent artists and potentially boost sales, additional lawsuits ensued.

In a 2001 legal settlement, the company agreed to pay copyright owners and record labels $26 million plus royalties. Napster declared bankruptcy in 2002, and shut down its services. Napster attempted a paid subscription service that was not successful. Napster was eventually bought out by electronics retailer Best Buy in 2008, which merged it with the music service Rhapsody in 2011.

remained the solid workhorse behind the operation, monitoring all aspects of Thefacebook and collecting data on how people were using the site.

It was not long before Parker got involved in the legal structure of Thefacebook. In July 2004, he filed papers to have the company incorporated in Delaware. The ownership was broken down so Parker and Moskovitz each owned between 6 and 7 percent of Thefacebook. Zuckerberg and Saverin's shares went down to 51 percent and 34.4 percent.

HOW ARE WE GOING TO PAY FOR THIS?

The new legal filing angered Saverin, as did the continued backlash against his ideas from Zuckerberg and Parker. Saverin froze the bank account in July so Zuckerberg had no access to the funds. Without another option, Zuckerberg went to his parents for help. He funneled a total of approximately $85,000 of family money into the company. Most of the money paid for servers to support the growth of 100,000 to 200,000 users over just three summer months.

Nervous Thefacebook would suffer from server overload like Friendster, Zuckerberg was very focused on maintaining its server capacity. The company

SERVERS

A server is a computer or device on a network that manages its resources. The term refers to both software and hardware, meaning either specific software running on a computer or the actual computer running the software. Many networks run off the client-server model, where each computer is either a client that runs applications or a server that manages resources such as data. The type of network determines the type of server used. Simple networks most likely use file and print servers. File servers store and retrieve files for users. Print servers send requests from a network computer to a specified printer. Database servers have both a front-end that serves up requested data and a back-end that handles data analysis and storage.

was now getting too big to pay for an outside company's servers—it needed its own network. Parker recruited an experienced engineer, Taner Halicioglu, to help manage Thefacebook network. The company set up its servers in Santa Clara, California, a 20-minute drive from the headquarters. The team went to add new servers every few days.

It was becoming clear that in order to pay for the servers and support growth to more schools, Thefacebook was going to have to seriously consider outside funding. Google had already shown interest in investing. Other companies and investors seemed anxious to get a piece of the company as well. But negotiations could be tricky. The next few months would test whether Zuckerberg was cut out for the role of CEO. +

Friendster became a social gaming site in June 2002.

The Winklevoss twins and Narendra accused Zuckerberg of stealing the idea for Thefacebook.

THIS IS SERIOUS BUSINESS

Zuckerberg and his partners mixed hard work and fun during their first summer in Palo Alto. There was a sense that they were on the brink of something about to explode. Unfortunately, the college lifestyle did not bode well for the rental house. The owners were not pleased with the condition and sued Thefacebook crew for damage to the property in September 2004.

By fall, Thefacebook team faced more than the property damage claim. Zuckerberg and Saverin were officially at odds, and the company was in flux. They could not agree on the best direction for the company. Zuckerberg increasingly wanted Saverin out of business dealings, while Saverin was fighting to maintain control.

Meanwhile, ConnectU filed a lawsuit against Zuckerberg in September. The Winklevoss brothers and Divya Narendra accused Zuckerberg of stealing the idea for Thefacebook. They argued that Zuckerberg had secretly used ideas for Thefacebook he took from the social networking site they hired him to build.

Amid the drama, Thefacebook continued its growth. The new school year meant there would be a lot more college students joining and using Thefacebook. The team

PALO ALTO, CALIFORNIA

The bike-friendly city of Palo Alto, California, is located near the Stanford University campus. It is also the epicenter of Silicon Valley. Major technology companies such as Hewlett-Packard and the popular Web site Pinterest, are headquartered in Palo Alto. A subsidiary of Amazon.com and several venture capital firms also reside there. The first Apple store opened in Palo Alto.

DIVYA NARENDRA

Divya Narendra started ConnectU with the Winklevoss brothers and was one of the defendants in the lawsuit against Zuckerberg. He has since gone on to found the investment network SumZero. As of 2012, he attended law school at Northwestern University.

needed additional staff and servers in order to meet the new demand.

MAINTAINING CONTROL

Thefacebook team had done a fine job building the Web site with no outside resources, but the company had grown too big to maintain itself without real investment. Still, Zuckerberg was wary of taking money from anyone who might try to control Thefacebook's destiny. Usually, when investors put a large amount of money into a start-up company, in exchange they get partial ownership of that company. The idea is that when the company grows and makes money, the investors will make back more than their investment, making a profit. Many investors negotiate for control over running the company in order to ensure the company will be successful and earn money. For example, investors might insist the company do business with another firm they own, or they might insist on choosing a new CEO to run the company.

Parker had learned the hard way that starting a company does not guarantee control of it forever. He did not want Zuckerberg to make the same mistake he did by letting control of Thefacebook end up in the wrong hands.

Parker scheduled a meeting with his friend, investor Reid Hoffman. Hoffman was familiar with social networking and already invested in LinkedIn, a professional social networking site. Hoffman introduced Zuckerberg and Parker to Peter Thiel. Thiel became an investor after founding and selling

THE SOCIAL NETWORK

In 2009, author Ben Mezrich released an unofficial exposé about Facebook, *The Accidental Billionaires: The Founding of Facebook: A Tale of Sex, Money, Genius, and Betrayal*. The book detailed the early days of Facebook and went on to become a best seller. Most of Mezrich's material came from interviews, including with Saverin, but the author never spoke to Zuckerberg when researching the book. Some critics have questioned the truth behind some events described in the book.

When asked about the book, Zuckerberg called it a work of fiction. "Honestly, I wish that when people tried to do journalism or write stuff about Facebook, they at least try to get it right," Zuckerberg said.[1]

The book was the basis for the 2010 film *The Social Network*, written by Aaron Sorkin and directed by David Fincher. Actor Jesse Eisenberg starred as Zuckerberg. The film received critical acclaim, as well as Academy Awards for Best Film Editing, Original Score, and Adapted Screenplay. It also received Academy Award nominations for Best Picture, Best Director, and Best Actor.

In a *CNBC* guest blog, Saverin wrote: "I hope that this film inspires countless others to create and take that leap to start a new business. With a little luck, you might even change the world."[2]

Hoffman was cofounder of LinkedIn and an early investor in Thefacebook.

the online payment site PayPal to eBay for
$1.5 billion.

As an entrepreneur, Thiel had a good nose
for sniffing out a company that had real promise.
While some investors worried that interest in
social networking would pass, Thiel recognized
Thefacebook's growth potential. The company had
attracted a lot of attention with only a relatively
small number of schools as members. What would
happen when it opened to more schools? What
would happen when it opened to the world outside
of college? He wanted in.

Thiel made a deal with Zuckerberg. He would
loan the company $500,000. The company would

not have to pay him back as long as Thefacebook held up its end of the bargain—to increase to 1.5 million users within six months of the investment. At that point, his investment would be converted to stock. Thiel's investment attracted an additional $100,000 from a few other investors. The company's value hit $4.9 million.

The best part of the deal was that Thiel was not interested in telling Zuckerberg how to run his company. Thiel's investment did secure him a seat on Thefacebook's board of directors. Parker occupied one seat, while Zuckerberg had control of two seats. With majority ownership of the company, Zuckerberg had managed to ensure he would continue to have the final say when it came to business matters concerning Thefacebook.

ONE MILLION USERS

With the loan from Thiel, Thefacebook quickly added new users. By the end of November, Thefacebook team held a party

PAYPAL AND PETER THIEL

The online auction site eBay acquired PayPal in 2002. Founder Peter Thiel resigned as CEO at the time of acquisition. A Stanford University graduate, Thiel is on *Forbes* magazine's 400 wealthiest people list as of September 2011, with a value of $1.5 billion. His Facebook stock alone is valued well over $1 billion as of February 2012. Among other Internet start-ups, Thiel invested in Yelp, Friendster, and LinkedIn.

celebrating 1 million users at Frisson, a swanky club owned by Thiel in San Francisco. Zuckerberg and his crew were living in a new rental house in Los Altos Hill, but they seemed to be outgrowing their college lifestyle quickly.

Thefacebook team began thinking about expanding the service outside the college market. The site had successfully expanded beyond the Ivy League to other universities in the United States. At many universities, "Facebook" was becoming a staple of student conversation. "I'll Facebook you" was a familiar phrase heard in university hallways, meaning, "I'll get in touch with you."

Advertising was expanding too. Thefacebook made a deal with Apple that brought in more than $50,000 a month. However, Apple did not want a standard banner advertisement along the top or the side of the Web site. Instead, Apple paid Thefacebook one dollar for each new member who joined an Apple group.

The investment had allowed Thefacebook to survive a crucial moment of growth during the fall of 2004. It was soon clear the company needed more money and infrastructure in order to succeed.

Thiel gave Thefacebook its first sound investment.

Washington Post Company CEO Graham is a Harvard graduate.

BIG INVESTMENT

Thefacebook was approaching its first birthday in February 2005. The tiny team had managed to start the company, keep it operational, grow the business, secure its first round of investment, and develop a board of directors. The team moved into its first office on Emerson Avenue in downtown Palo Alto. Thefacebook now had well over 1 million users, and many of them were logging onto the site every day. New opportunities to expand the business were coming from every direction. It was time for Zuckerberg and his business partners to consider a second investment.

Zuckerberg knew a Harvard University classmate who worked in the investment branch of the Washington Post Company. The Post invited Zuckerberg in for a meeting, and he brought Parker. They met the CEO, Don Graham, a somewhat older gentleman who had also graduated from Harvard. He was impressed by Zuckerberg and Thefacebook, and the two hit it off immediately. Zuckerberg felt he could trust Graham, and Graham made it clear the Post was interested in investing in Thefacebook right off the bat.

Thefacebook's meeting with the Post sent a flurry through the venture capitalist community. Pretty soon, Viacom, owner of Music Television (MTV) and Paramount Pictures, was ready to make a bid to buy Thefacebook. Both companies were willing to spend $75 million. News Corporation, their largest competitor, had already purchased MySpace. Viacom desperately wanted a social networking site to pair Web content with MTV programming. Soon, however, it became clear Zuckerberg did not want to sell his company.

Zuckerberg was not easily swayed by dollar signs. Investors would need to propose a partnership in which Zuckerberg maintained control of Thefacebook. Even though Thefacebook and its CEO were young, the company had a solid bargaining position.

While Thefacebook fielded proposals, venture capital firm Accel Partners came out of nowhere to make an offer. Accel was willing to put a big offer forward after losing out on other major investment opportunities in Web sites such as Flickr. Zuckerberg was torn after seriously considering a partnership with the Post. Having grown close to Graham, Zuckerberg called him for his advice. While it meant the Post would miss out on a big opportunity, Graham told Zuckerberg to go with Accel. The event solidified a friendship between Graham and Zuckerberg.

In the end, Accel had the winning bid. The company invested $12.7 million in Thefacebook in May 2005. Thefacebook left the meeting with a new valuation of nearly $98 million, an unthinkable figure for such a new company. The investment officially ousted Saverin from Thefacebook, and he no longer had an official position with the company. His percentage share dropped from more than 34 percent to 10 percent. Zuckerberg had become a millionaire at age 20.

HEY! COME WORK FOR US!

Thefacebook had new money and new goals, and now it needed a new team fast. Many experienced Silicon Valley executives remained a bit wary of Thefacebook's youthful reputation despite the press and its stunning financial position. It would take a few missteps before the right team was in place. The company's first hire was Steve Chen as vice president of engineering. Chen quit within a few weeks to start the video-sharing site YouTube.

Thefacebook had been working with Tricia Black from

EDUARDO SAVERIN

Original Thefacebook investor Eduardo Saverin owned approximately 5 percent of Thefacebook valued at more than $2.5 billion as of 2011. His original shares were diluted during Thefacebook's investment rounds. Saverin pursued a lawsuit against the company that was eventually settled out of court. As part of the settlement, he cannot speak publicly about Facebook. As of 2011, Saverin lives in Singapore and continues to invest in start-up companies. One company was Qwiki, an online search engine that provides multimedia rather than link-based content in response to Web queries. In March 2011, Saverin invested $6.5 million in a company called Jumio. Jumio creates image recognition technology that enables devices to read and understand information from video streams.

YOUTUBE

YouTube is a video hosting Web site that allows users to upload videos, as well as view and comment on videos posted by others. It was founded by Steve Chen, Chad Hurley, and Jawed Karim in 2005. The three founders met as employees at PayPal. The first video, called "Me at the zoo," was uploaded by Karim on April 23, 2005. It shows Karim in front of the elephant cage at the San Diego Zoo. Google purchased YouTube in October 2006 for $1.65 billion. Hurley and Chen were ranked twenty-eighth on CNN's list of the 50 People Who Matter in 2006.

YouTube hit 4 billion daily views in January 2012, and the company estimates 60 hours of video are uploaded every minute. John Cloud wrote in *Time* magazine in 2006: "YouTube is to video browsing what a Wal-Mart Supercenter is to shopping: everything is there, and all you have to do is walk in the door."[1]

There have been multiple instances of previously unknown events or people, such as singer Justin Bieber, becoming overnight YouTube sensations. This usually occurs when a video goes viral. A YouTube video can be viewed by millions of people in a very short amount of time, with links transmitted via e-mail across the world and posted to Facebook profiles.

Y2M and eventually hired her to run the new advertising department. Accel suggested Thefacebook hire Jeff Rothschild as a part-time consultant in the spring of 2005. Rothschild was a retiree from Veritas, a business software company. His much younger colleagues at Thefacebook had fun trying to make him hip, nicknaming him "J-Ro" and getting him to wear designer jeans. Additionally, Stanford graduate Paul Janzer led a customer service department set up to field user questions and complaints. Moskovitz and D'Angelo returned from the original group.

Other new hires tended to be very young and somewhat unexpected—Thefacebook actively preferred college dropouts to high-achieving scholars. In some cases, the company even encouraged potential hires to drop out, promising to pay their tuition at a later date if they immediately came to work for Thefacebook.

One notable new hire was a college graduate. Ruchi Sanghvi became the first female engineer to work at Thefacebook. Sanghvi was a Carnegie-Mellon graduate and helped Moskovitz keep the site running smoothly.

With higher standards to maintain, Zuckerberg and partners began viewing every mistake more critically. One bug in late 2005 temporarily allowed Thefacebook users to easily hack into each other's accounts. This sort of security breach could devastate a social network and caused the team to briefly panic. Luckily, Moskovitz swiftly solved the problem in his typical collected fashion with no serious damage done.

One mistake did not have such an easy fix. In late summer 2005, Parker was arrested for drug possession while out of town on vacation. No official

Sanghvi, *left*, was the first female engineer to work at Thefacebook.

charges were made, but investors were extremely concerned the incident involving a partner would tarnish Thefacebook's reputation. An agreement determined Parker would leave Thefacebook, give up half of his stock options, and vacate his board seat. He decided to give that seat to Zuckerberg, granting the young CEO even more power as "hereditary king of Facebook."[2]

A MAN AND A COMPANY WITH A VISION

Few members of Thefacebook team had business degrees or training. Zuckerberg especially needed education on basic business dealings. He began seeking out friends in the technology community in order to learn important skills as CEO. In addition to Graham, Marc Andreessen, founder of the Internet browser Netscape, became another mentor to Zuckerberg.

Zuckerberg's mentors inspired him to develop and communicate a strategic vision to the rest of the world. To successfully run the company, it was important for Zuckerberg's message to motivate his team and also inspire the site's millions of users. Zuckerberg kept

NETSCAPE VS. MICROSOFT

Netscape Communications was a legendary Silicon Valley start-up and one of the first ventures to embrace the launch of the Internet in the mid-1990s. Founded in 1994, Netscape was the joint venture of Jim Clark and Marc Andreessen. Netscape dominated the browser market until Microsoft Corporation's almost identical browser, Internet Explorer, surpassed it. Microsoft licensed Internet Explorer and bundled it with its successful Windows operating system. The battle between Microsoft and Netscape was known informally in Silicon Valley as the Browser Wars. Netscape could no longer compete from a marketing or financial standpoint. AOL purchased Netscape in 1999. As of 2007, the browser was no longer updated.

notes and plans for this vision in a book called the "Book of Change." That is where crucial moves made by Thefacebook were first recorded.

As Zuckerberg was starting to grow up, the company also changed its name. In September 2005, Thefacebook became simply Facebook. It had a new name and a new look, but the site remained simple and unflashy—easily recognizable by its original users. +

Zuckerberg has resolved to maintain control of Facebook.

Facebook had $9 million in revenue in 2005.

NEW DIRECTIONS FOR A NEW COMPANY

Facebook had passed the threshold to become a legitimate company in 2005. The technology community no longer assumed Facebook would be bought and absorbed by a larger corporation. With its new status and new name, Facebook decided

it was the right time to make a statement about its vision for the future.

The question, "What is Facebook?" might result in different answers. Author David Kirkpatrick wrote in *The Facebook Effect* that Zuckerberg called Facebook a "Directory of the People." Parker referred to it as "a device you carried around and pointed at people so it would tell you all about them."[1] Regardless of how it was described, one of Facebook's most powerful aspects was its network effects. This meant it gained more importance—and more value—as more people used it. It also meant Facebook had to make sure its users were happy and logging in every day. It was vital that more new users signed up all the time.

New users meant opening up Facebook to people outside of college, such as high school students. The Facebook team, however, was nervous that allowing the younger group in would alienate its college base. But it turned out to not make much difference to existing users when Facebook opened the site to high school students in September 2005. That is because the Facebook experience depends on the network each user builds for themselves. Initially, the high school and college services were kept separate, but they eventually merged. One

EFFECTS OF SOCIAL NETWORKING ON KIDS

Because Facebook and other sites are widely used by kids and teenagers, some professionals have speculated about how it affects their development. Psychologists have identified a number of possible negative affects linking overuse to antisocial behavior, narcissism, anxiety, and depression. Some of these connections could be related to physical inactivity because kids spend too much time on Facebook instead of exercising or playing outdoors. Psychologists have also observed that Facebook can cause increased distraction among kids, which could negatively impact academic performance.

Perhaps the biggest threat to the psychological well-being of adolescents is cyberbullying, when peers use social networking sites to post negative or harmful things about less popular classmates. Relentless cyberbullying has been connected to several incidents of teen suicides.

Social networking can also have positive effects on kids. In one study, kids who used Facebook a lot showed more "virtual empathy."[2] Social networking also helped shy kids interact with their peers in the digital space. Psychologists have also recognized that social networks have developed many multimedia learning tools.

million high school users were on Facebook by April 2006. Facebook eventually opened to all users in February 2006. Meanwhile, Zuckerberg closed a third round of financing for Facebook, an investment of $27.5 million that increased the company's value to $500 million.

A PICTURE SPEAKS 1,000 WORDS

One reason behind Facebook's network effects was its users generated most of the content on the site. But what would make people continue to go to Facebook to view

new content? What would make users continue to create content worth viewing? The answer—or at least one of several answers—was photos. Facebook introduced a feature that allowed users to upload photos in October 2005.

The team observed that users spent most of their time on Facebook looking at their friends' photos, especially those that were recently uploaded. Flickr, a photo hosting site, created "tagging," where a photographer could insert a label for a photo based on its content. The Facebook team introduced tagging on the site in late October to make it easier for users to view the photos of their friends. Users can tag the names of their friends in a photo. Tags are clickable, making it easy to move from one photo album to the next. Pretty soon, people were uploading hundreds of photos to Facebook. One month after the photo feature launched, 85 percent of Facebook users were tagged in at least one photo.

THEY HATE IT!

Another Facebook feature, the News Feed, was not an immediate hit. In September 2006, Facebook unveiled the News Feed and considered it a major game changer in the social networking world.

Information

Group Info

Name: Students against Facebook News Feed (Official Petition to Facebook)

Type: Common Interest - Philosophy

Description: You went a bit too far this time, facebook. Very few of us want everyone automatically knowing what we update. We want to feel just a LITTLE bit of privacy, even if it is facebook. News Feed is just too creepy, too stalker-esque, and a feature that has to go.

We demand that either the feature goes, or that we have an option to remove ourselves from the feature. Nothing people write on our walls, or what we write, or what we update goes up on the "News Feed." These are small demands of your users, but we are here to complain and protect our privacy.

I know it's odd to protest facebook through facebook, but this perhaps is the best way for them to get the message.

Until this feature is removed or changed to protect my privacy, I WILL NOT update my profile, and I hope you will too.

Students Against Facebook News Feed

Facebook users formed groups opposed to the News Feed.

Zuckerberg and his team had planned the News Feed for eight months. A team was dedicated to developing timesorting, a feature where users could view the most recently updated profiles and photos. Timesorting gathered data to determine which profiles users looked at the most. This data was entered into Facebook's system so users could easily access the most recent activity or what the site thought users found interesting based on their activity.

Facebook launched the News Feed on user home pages, which appeared as a reel listing their friends' most recent activity, such as "Sarah uploaded a new photo," or "Phil is now friends with Sarah."

Users no longer had to click through profiles to find new content. Zuckerberg was convinced the News Feed brought a tremendous new value to users, so he was shocked when they hated it.

The News Feed did not display content that was not already public on Facebook. But it provided this content to users in a much more direct and open way. It made many users extremely uncomfortable, some said browsing Facebook was similar to stalking. Soon, user complaints were populating Facebook's blog.

Although Facebook users wrote about their dislike for the News Feed, the team discovered the feature created more activity on the site. With the News Feed, people were logging in more often, clicking through more pages, and staying on for longer sessions. Rather than remove it, Zuckerberg decided to keep the News Feed alive. However, he apologized for not warning users in advance, and Facebook set up new settings that helped users control the personal

RUCHI SANGHVI

Ruchi Sanghvi made news—and was personally attacked—after penning the Facebook blog post, "Facebook Gets a Facelift," announcing the News Feed in 2006. Sanghvi wrote: "News Feed and Mini-Feed are a different way of looking at the news about your friends, but they do not give out any information that wasn't already visible. . . . We hope these changes help you stay more up to date on your friends' lives."[3] The Carnegie-Mellon graduate was called the "devil" among other insults by angry Facebook users.[4]

VIRGIN AIRLINES

Inappropriate Facebook activity has caused many users to be fired from their jobs. In one incident, 13 Virgin Airlines crewmembers were fired after they used Facebook to discuss private information about the plane's equipment, claimed cockroaches had infested the cabins, and made insulting remarks about the airline's passengers.

information available to their network. Zuckerberg's handling of the difficult situation gained him new respect from his staff and the public.

STICKING TO THE PLAN

One reason Zuckerberg did not remove the News Feed was it brought activity to the site, despite users' complaints. But he also recognized that the News Feed was launched before users were ready. The News Feed feature was also fundamental to Zuckerberg's strategic vision for Facebook to become a platform for other applications. The only way that could happen was to share user activity openly and on a timely basis.

The drama around News Feed highlighted one of the core debates surrounding Facebook. Most users want to stay updated about their friends and their communities. But people are uncomfortable with publicly exposing their private business. Personal information becoming public is particularly true when it comes to the Internet. +

The launch of the News Feed raised privacy concerns among users.

Zuckerberg speaks at the first f8 Conference in 2007.

LOOKING AT REVENUE

By the end of 2006, Facebook was becoming more stable, unveiling its Share feature in November. With Share, users could share links by clicking the Facebook icon on more than 20 partner Web sites, including *Time*, the *Wall Street*

Journal, and the photo sharing site Photobucket. Users could select how to share a link and who to share it with, including people who were not on Facebook.

Investors started asking how to make more money to support the company's continued growth. Zuckerberg had always shied away from traditional advertising and disliked the idea of littering Facebook with product images or anything else that disrupted the user experience. Facebook turned down beverage company Sprite's $1 million offer in 2006 to turn the home page green for one day because it would disrupt the usability of the site.

But Facebook started to see that advertising could add value for users and also help companies attract customers in new ways. Zuckerberg turned down more offers from Yahoo! Inc., AOL, Time Warner, and Viacom to sell Facebook. Instead, Facebook used the publicity to lock down an important advertising deal with Microsoft, bringing in $100 million in revenue per year. The company ended 2006 with a recorded $48 million in revenue and 12 million monthly active users.

WHAT'S IN A PLATFORM?

Zuckerberg admired Microsoft's ability to create a platform for software. Similarly, he wanted Facebook to become a platform for communication. As a platform, Facebook could easily partner with other technology companies, rather than compete with them. The company planned to unveil itself as a platform on May 24, 2007, at the first Facebook f8 conference in San Francisco, California. The event was a conference for developers and its name, f8, "subtly proclaimed it was Facebook's 'fate' to become a platform."[1]

Facebook engineers and staff worked tirelessly for days to prepare for f8. It was one of the largest events in the company's history. As Zuckerberg introduced the event, there was a noticeable sense of excitement in the air. Zuckerberg announced, "Together we're starting a movement."[2]

Facebook revealed hundreds of applications that were built on the site, including games and utilities. The transition of Facebook into a platform for applications caught on quickly. Within six months of f8, developers created 25,000 applications. Facebook gained more respect in Silicon Valley as a serious technology company.

But many applications were not considered useful, and, in Zuckerberg's view, clogged the network. Zuckerberg hoped more applications would serve an important purpose, like Causes, which helped users raise money for the causes they cared about. But many applications were downright trivial. Facebook decided to clean up the applications by developing a rating system. The rating system had specified guidelines to help Facebook verify which applications were worthwhile and those that were not.

FRIENDS FOREVER: MICROSOFT AND FACEBOOK

With more growth opportunities than ever before, Facebook ramped up for another round of financing. Zuckerberg believed Facebook's value was around $20 billion. Major companies were once again

MICROSOFT CORPORATION

Microsoft Corporation was founded in 1975 by Bill Gates and Paul Allen, after they converted a common computer programming language, BASIC, for use on a personal computer (PC). Gates and Allen were childhood friends from Seattle, Washington. International Business Machines Corporation (IBM) hired Microsoft to develop an operating system for its first PC in 1980. Microsoft developed Microsoft Disk Operating System (MS-DOS), which was sold with the IBM PC in 1981, and quickly rose to dominance in the home computer industry. Microsoft is based in Redmond, Washington, and recorded almost $70 billion in revenue in 2011. Gates is also well-known for his charitable work after starting the Bill & Melinda Gates Foundation in 1994. The organization contributes to many global health initiatives.

interested in buying Facebook, including Google and Microsoft.

Zuckerberg decided to retain control of his company. Instead, Peter Thiel negotiated an investment deal with Microsoft CEO Steve Ballmer. In October, Microsoft invested $240 million in exchange for 1.6 percent ownership of Facebook. The new deal specified that Facebook could not take any investments from Google, making Google and Facebook clear competitors. The investment put Facebook's valuation at $15 billion. It also meant Microsoft would have the first option to buy Facebook if Zuckerberg ever decided to sell it.

REVENUE STRATEGIES

At an event for advertisers in November, Facebook announced the launch of Facebook Pages and self-service advertising. It was a multifaceted advertising strategy that created conversations and involvement with users. Through Facebook Pages, companies could create their own pages for free, and any user could click to become a "fan." Part of the idea behind Pages was that companies would advertise on Facebook once they created their page and started gaining fans. One advertising campaign

Microsoft CEO Ballmer negotiated a deal that solidified Microsoft's relationship with Facebook.

for Procter & Gamble's Crest Whitening Strips offered users a chance to win movie and concert tickets if they joined the product's Facebook page. Quickly, 20,000 new users joined.

FACEBOOK BEACON INCIDENTS

There were several incidents with users that caused Facebook Beacon to backfire. A Massachusetts man purchased a ring from Overstock.com, which showed up in his News Feed, "Sean Lane bought 14k White Gold 1/5 ct Diamond Eternity Flower Ring from overstock.com."[3] Lane's wife sent him a message asking who the ring was for. The ring was meant to be a Christmas present for her. Another man purchased a movie ticket, and a notification was posted in his News Feed from Fandango.com. The man's girlfriend became upset because he had previously agreed to take her to the same movie the next week.

Self-service advertisements used site-collected information to direct advertisements that were the most relevant to specific users. For example, an ad for a digital camera might be displayed only to people with kids who have not posted any photographs to the site.

FACEBOOK BEACON

Part of the new advertising strategy was the Facebook Beacon, which allowed participating companies to post alerts of users' activity onto their friends' News Feed. One issue with Beacon was that users were not explicitly asked if they wanted to publish the information to Facebook. Many felt Beacon was invasive and misused their personal information so Facebook could make money. Author David Kirkpatrick wrote,

But while it was intended for activities like playing a game

or adding a recipe to an online recipe box, it also could be used to announce purchases you made on partner sites.[4]

Similar to the News Feed launch, the Beacon service put Facebook in the center of a much larger discussion about maintaining control of personal identity in the digital age. Facebook had the philosophy of radical transparency. This philosophy meant that a community not only benefits from openly exchanging information, it is actually safer for people to be completely open rather than hide through social networks. In a sense, this viewpoint argues that Facebook makes the world a safer place.

SHERYL SANDBERG

The controversy with Facebook Beacon made it clear that it was crucial for Facebook to have a leader with experience and knowledge to develop a successful advertising strategy. That leader was Sheryl Sandberg. When Sandberg joined Facebook in March 2008, the company was "missing the layer right below the senior-executive team."[5] Zuckerberg first met Sandberg at a party when she was working as a senior executive for Google. Though the two of them were very different—Sandberg was a mother of two in

Facebook COO Sandberg was previously a vice president at Google.

her forties who favored designer clothing as much as Zuckerberg preferred T-shirts—they hit it off right away. Zuckerberg offered Sandberg the position of chief operating officer (COO), meaning she was in charge of all of Facebook's operations.

Even with the anti-advertising culture at Facebook, Sandberg was determined to get the team excited about new revenue-building initiatives. She started by holding regular meetings with company decision makers. She wanted the team to consider what Facebook brought to its users in order to identify how to create new marketplace demands.

This resulted in new revenue-generating ideas, such as Facebook Credits. Facebook Credits are virtual currency that can be used toward virtual goods in Facebook applications or games. One dollar is the equivalent of ten Facebook Credits. Facebook Credits can be purchased with a credit card or through the payment service PayPal. An example of this is purchasing gold coins in the

ZYNGA

Social game start-up company Zynga has had the most success creating applications for Facebook. These include Texas HoldEm Poker, a Facebook version of poker, FarmVille, and Mafia Wars. Zynga is considered to be one of the most profitable companies in history, all from building on Facebook's platform. Part of this success is Zynga's sales of virtual goods, which do not cost much to make and the company does not have to ship. With a reported revenue of $1.4 billion in 2011, Mark Pincus is Zynga's CEO. Former MySpace CEO and former Facebook COO Owen Van Natta is on the company's board of directors.

WINKLEVOSS TWINS

Twin brothers Tyler and Cameron Winklevoss led an extensive and much-publicized lawsuit against Thefacebook. It was settled in 2008 for $65 million, partially based on the value of Facebook stock. The brothers believed the stock had been undervalued at the time and attempted to reopen the case in 2010, hoping to increase their final payment to as much as half a billion dollars. When the court of appeals rejected the request, the Winklevosses briefly threatened to take the case to the Supreme Court. This action was later withdrawn.

The Winklevoss twins also sued the law firm that represented them against Zuckerberg, Quinn Emanuel Urquhart & Sullivan, for malpractice. They attempted to have the $13 million in contingency fees they owed the firm excused. Their argument was that the firm made the $65 million settlement with Facebook public, which violated confidentiality. They lost the case at the New York Supreme Court level.

Aside from the lawsuit, the Winklevoss twins are best known for their accomplishments in rowing. They competed in the 2008 Olympic Games in Beijing but did not qualify for the semifinals. After the Olympics, the Winklevoss twins attended the University of Oxford to pursue master of business associate degrees.

popular Facebook game Farmville, which was developed by Zynga. Instead of displaying banners on the site, users could participate in contests or conversations on fan pages. Other revenue came from virtual goods, with users buying digital balloons or flowers to give a friend.

The combined approach to revenue building led by Sandberg has been enormously successful. Meanwhile, Zuckerberg found a trusted partner whose skills differ from but complement his own strengths as a leader.

INTERNAL CHANGES

In June 2008, Facebook's ongoing legal battle with the ConnectU founders officially ended. Facebook settled with the Winklevoss twins and Narendra for an undisclosed amount.

At the same time, several members of Facebook's core group departed in 2008. Facebook cofounder Hughes left to work on Barack Obama's 2008 Presidential campaign and later founded Jumo, a nonprofit organization. D'Angelo and Charlie Cheever, one of Facebook's top engineers, also left to start Quora, a question-and-answer Web site.

Perhaps the most bittersweet loss for Zuckerberg was the departure of cofounder Moskovitz, who had devoted himself to the company from the very beginning. Moskovitz started a company called Asana, a business communication

ADAM D'ANGELO AND QUORA.COM

Adam D'Angelo started the Web site Quora.com with another ex-Facebook employee, Charlie Cheever, in 2009. The site is designed to help users get information and answers to questions from trusted sources by aggregating people by their interests. These sources could be practicing experts such as doctors, economists, or military veterans. Users create profiles that store and make easily visible all the topics they want to know more about. Quora.com is based in Palo Alto and valued at more than $1 billion. Cheever and D'Angelo were listed in inc.com's 30 Under 30 list in 2011. Quora.com launched its first iPhone application in September 2011. Since then, Facebook launched a competitive product called Facebook Questions.

and workplace organization application. He also continued to create software that can be used through Facebook's network. No longer surrounded by his college pals, Zuckerberg continued in his mission to make Facebook a global phenomenon. +

Moskovitz, a technical workhorse behind Facebook, left in 2008.

Through Places, Facebook users could check in at a location using their smartphones.

FACEBOOK, A GLOBAL PHENOMENON

By 2009, Facebook had gone from a Harvard dorm room to becoming a fixture in its users' lives. It became the primary way people stay in touch with each other and provided companies with a necessary mechanism to reach their consumers.

With more than 600 million users in November 2010, much of Facebook's growth occurred in developing countries in the Middle East and Southeast Asia. In fact, more than 75 percent of active Facebook users lived outside the United States. The service is available in at least 75 languages.

Facebook offered users even more ways to come together by the end of 2010. Facebook launched a new version of Facebook Groups, allowing members to create pages for "important groups of people in your life— your family, your soccer team, your book club."[1] Another feature was Facebook Places, where users could check in at a location using the geotagging feature on their smartphones. Places was considered a failure, however, and was discontinued in 2011. Sam Biddle of *Gizmodo* wrote that users preferred Foursquare, a location-based Web site and application, over Places. Users could check-in via their smartphones and post it on their Facebook profiles. "Places was

GEOTAGGING

Many applications created for Facebook, mobile devices, and tablets provide geotagging features that locate the application's user. Geotags can link to other content near the location. Geotagging has been used widely in mapping devices, such as GPS navigation systems, which provide audio directions in automobiles to help drivers get from one location to the next. Geotagging is also a feature used in many photo sorting applications and services.

FACEBOOK EMPLOYEE PERKS

Facebook has adopted many of the employee perks that technology start-up companies such as Google have used to motivate their staff and keep them happy. These perks include flexible work hours, ample vacation time, and childcare reimbursement. Free shuttles to and from the Menlo Park campus and reimbursements for public transportation are available to employees. Breakfast, lunch, dinner, beverages, and snacks are all provided free of charge in the college dormitory-style cafeteria.

simply superfluous. . . . So it just sat there, unnecessary, awkward, a quiet second fiddle," Biddle wrote.[2]

MAINTAINING FEATURES AND PRIVACY

At Facebook's September 2011 f8 conference, the company unveiled an updated version of the Facebook Profile called Timeline. Events, photos, and posts are displayed on profiles as a timeline of when they were created. Facebook also announced that through Open Graph Application Programming Interfaces (APIs) developers are capable of creating social applications for sharing and self-expression.

After years of moving from one building to the next, the Facebook team officially moved into new headquarters in Menlo Park, California, in December 2011. The new office campus, formerly the home of Sun Microsystems, sits on 57 acres (23 ha) and houses 2,000 employees. John Tenanes, Facebook's

The new Facebook Timeline tells the story of a user's life, as it is recorded on Facebook.

global director of real estate, wrote in a Facebook blog post that a central courtyard connects the nine buildings on the new campus. There are no private offices or cubicles, he said: "This is because we believe transparency and openness help us move fast, even as we grow."[3]

That transparency has extended to how Facebook has handled mounting privacy issues. Between 2010 and 2011, Facebook created 20 distinct tools offering users more control over privacy settings, including tools for choosing who can view certain posts and reviewing tags on photos or posts.

In 2011, the US Federal Trade Commission and Facebook agreed to privacy guidelines for large technology companies that have access to private user data. Facebook also hired a management team for security and privacy, with Erin Egan as chief privacy officer of policy and Michael Richter as chief privacy officer of products.

INSTANT MILLIONAIRES

The Facebook IPO made a lot of people even richer, such as its four founders. Zuckerberg owns the largest share of Facebook, 28.2 percent, and made an estimated $19.2 billion from his company's IPO. Moskovitz made $5.1 billion from his 5 percent stake, and Hughes made an estimated $835 million from his 1 percent. Despite being pushed out of the company, Saverin made $2.7 billion from his estimated 5 percent share. Parker owns 4 percent, equaling an estimated $3.4 billion.

But a number of people became overnight millionaires who are not Facebook executives or its key investors. Among them are approximately 1,000 of the 3,000 Facebook employees. This includes David Choe, a graffiti artist who was hired to spray paint murals at Facebook's first Palo Alto offices in 2005. Originally, Facebook offered him $60,000 for the work. However, Choe chose to be paid for the job in Facebook stock, rather than cash. Choe made an estimated $144.2 million from his 3.77 million shares.

GOING PUBLIC

Facebook sent ripples through the investment community once again when it filed for public offering on February 1, 2012. The process of going public refers to a company's stock being available for public purchase through the stock market. Facebook wanted to raise an initial public offering (IPO) of $16 billion, and the company was valued at $104 billion.

Facebook's filing with the Securities and Exchange Commission revealed interesting facts the company. The site has 845 million active users. They upload 250 million photos per day and make 2.7 billion likes and comments per day. Facebook earned $3.71 billion in 2011, and 12 percent of that came from the Zynga games offered on the site.

The NASDAQ began trading Facebook stock under the ticker symbol FB on May 18, 2012. Zuckerberg rang Wall Street's opening bell from Facebook headquarters in Menlo Park. For Facebook, it was an eagerly awaited opening day surrounded by much speculation among investors.

However, the Facebook stock price ended its first day of trading at $38.37, down from its opening price of $42. The price dipped below $30 by the end of May 2012. Many analysts

IPO FALLOUT

Facebook's disappointing debut led to questions about how it was handled. Several investors filed lawsuits against Facebook, Zuckerberg, and investment banking firm Morgan Stanley. Morgan Stanley was the main underwriter for the IPO, responsible for accurately assessing the value of Facebook's shares. Facebook allegedly cautioned Morgan Stanley and other banks prior to the IPO that its future revenues would be lower than previously projected. Morgan Stanley allegedly shared this information with preferred clients but withheld it from other investors. Most financial analysts concluded that Morgan Stanley overvalued and overestimated public demand for shares. As of May 2012, Wall Street regulators and the SEC were investigating the failed IPO, which had cost individual investors an estimated $630 million.

ZUCKERBERG, FACEBOOK'S LEADER

Zuckerberg keeps his own life rather private on Facebook. His profile has fairly limited content and paints the picture of a typical 20-something-year-old. Few would guess by his lifestyle that Zuckerberg is a billionaire. Zuckerberg changed his relationship status from "single" to "married" on May 19, 2012. The day after Facebook's IPO, Zuckerberg married his girlfriend of nine years, Priscilla Chan, in the backyard of their home in Palo Alto. Chan had graduated from medical school at the University of California at San Francisco just five days earlier. Zuckerberg and Chan were married in front of 100 guests, who thought they were attending a graduation party for Chan.

concluded the company's Wall Street debut was a flop. One reason was the lack of individual investors, who worried Facebook was a fad. Another was the perceived disinterest from Zuckerberg, who wore his trademark hoodie to a pre-IPO meeting with investors. One analyst called it a "mark of immaturity."[5]

While Facebook's IPO was considered a bust, Chunka Mui of *Forbes* argued the company itself is not: "While many might consider Facebook a fad, hundreds of millions of users do not and they are more engaged with Facebook than any other company in the world."[6]

For Facebook, it looks as though this is only the beginning. As Zuckerberg said, "We can look into the future and we can see what might exist—and it's going to be really, really good."[7]

Facebook's iconic like button appears on the sign for the company's
Menlo Park headquarters.

TIMELINE

1982	1983	1984
Eduardo Saverin is born in Sao Paulo, Brazil, on March 13.	Chris Hughes is born in Hickory, North Carolina, on November 26.	Mark Zuckerberg is born in Dobbs Ferry, New York, on May 14.

2004	2004	2004
Zuckerberg and Thefacebook team relocate to Palo Alto, California, in June.	Thefacebook secures its first major investment in June. Sean Parker becomes president of Thefacebook.	The creators of ConnectU file a federal lawsuit against Zuckerberg in September.

1984

2004

2004

Dustin Moskovitz is born in Gainesville, Florida, on May 22.

On February 4, Zuckerberg, Saverin, Hughes, and Moskovitz launch Thefacebook at Harvard University.

In June, Saverin secures Thefacebook's first partnership with advertising company Y2M.

2004

2005

2005

Thefacebook reaches 1 million users in November.

Thefacebook secures a second round of financing of $12.7 million in May.

Thefacebook officially changes its name to Facebook in September.

TIMELINE

2005

In September, Facebook allows high school users to join the site.

2005

Facebook introduces photos and photo tagging in October.

2006

In February, Facebook becomes open to the general public for users over age 13.

2007

Microsoft invests $240 million in the company in exchange for 1.6 percent ownership of Facebook.

2008

Facebook hires Sheryl Sandberg as COO in March.

2008

In June, Facebook settles the lawsuit with ConnectU out of court for a reported $65 million.

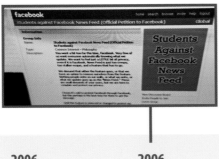

2006

The company raises $27.5 million in financing, increasing its valuation to $500 million.

2006

Facebook launches the News Feed in September.

2007

Facebook announces at f8 its new strategic direction as a platform for external applications by developers.

2008

Moskovitz, Facebook's oldest employee next to Zuckerberg, resigns.

2010

The Social Network film is released in theaters.

2012

Facebook becomes a publicly traded company in May.

ESSENTIAL FACTS

CREATORS

Chris Hughes (November 26, 1983–)

Dustin Moskovitz (May 22, 1984–)

Eduardo Saverin (March 13, 1982–)

Mark Zuckerberg (May 14, 1984–)

DATE LAUNCHED

February 4, 2004

CHALLENGES

After it first launched, Facebook's competitors included other social networking sites such as MySpace. As the site developed beyond a social database and into a platform, large technology-based corporations such as Google represented more significant competition. One of Facebook's main features, the News Feed, was not well received by users when it was introduced in 2006. Zuckerberg decided to keep the feature active, and it became crucial to Facebook's ability to provide a platform for multiple applications. Zuckerberg was sued by Cameron and Tyler Winklevoss and Divya Narendra for stealing the idea for Facebook from ConnectU. The case was settled out of court for $65 million in 2008.

SUCCESSES

Zuckerberg has managed to maintain control of Facebook and three seats on the board of directors even with multiple investment offers. This grants Zuckerberg an unusual amount of power and influence in the company. Since allowing users to tag one another in photos,

Facebook is now the Web's largest photo sharing site, with millions of photos uploaded every day. Facebook has developed into a platform where many other applications can be built and accessed through the site. Users can now pay bills, read newspaper articles, share photos, and support charitable causes through Facebook.

IMPACT ON SOCIETY

Facebook has been the focus of much public speculation about how social networking affects our culture. The debate centers around whether profiles put users' privacy at risk or if society should embrace radical transparency. As the world's number one social networking site, Facebook has become an important political tool that organizations and campaigns use to mobilize followers.

QUOTE

"By giving people the power to share, we're making the world more transparent."

—*Mark Zuckerberg*

GLOSSARY

application
> Computer software designed to help the user perform tasks.

confidante
> Person to whom private matters are confided.

digital
> Electronic, especially computerized, information.

entrepreneur
> The owner or manager of a business enterprise who, by risk and initiative, attempts to make profits.

exclusive
> Belonging to a particular individual or group and to no other; not shared.

financier
> One who deals with finance and investment on a large scale.

inventory
> To take stock of; evaluate.

legitimate
> In accordance with established rules, principles, or standards.

negotiate
> To arrange for or bring about by discussion and settlement of terms.

smartphone

A mobile phone with computerlike features including e-mail, Internet, and a personal organizer.

software

The programs used to direct the operations of a computer.

start-up

A young business enterprise.

timesorting

Gathering data to determine which profiles users looked at the most.

valuation

An estimated value or worth.

venture capital

Money invested or available for investment in the ownership of a new enterprise.

viral

Something quickly popularized by person-to-person electronic communication.

ADDITIONAL RESOURCES

SELECTED BIBLIOGRAPHY

Kirkpatrick, David. *The Facebook Effect*. New York: Simon & Schuster, 2010. Print.

Rosen, Larry. "Social Networking Good and Bad Impacts on Kids." *American Psychological Association*. American Psychological Association, 2011. Web. 25 Dec. 2011.

Wallace, James. *Hard Drive*. New York: John Wiley & Sons, 2007. Print.

FURTHER READINGS

Lusted, Marcia Amidon. *Social Networking: MySpace, Facebook, & Twitter*. Minneapolis, MN: ABDO, 2011. Print.

Powell, Rebecca. *YouTube: The Company and Its Founders*. Minneapolis, MN: ABDO, 2011. Print.

WEB LINKS

To learn more about Facebook, visit ABDO Publishing Company online at **www.abdopublishing.com**. Web sites about Facebook are featured on our Book Links page. These links are routinely monitored and updated to provide the most current information available.

PLACES TO VISIT

Computer History Museum
1401 N. Shoreline Boulevard
Mountain View, CA 94043
650-810-1010
www.computerhistory.org/
The Computer History Museum is the world's premier museum documenting and exploring the history of computing and its impact on society.

The Tech Museum
201 South Market Street
San Jose, CA 95113
408-294-8324
www.thetech.org
The Tech Museum has hundreds of exhibits relating to science and technology.

SOURCE NOTES

CHAPTER 1. $10 MILLION? NO THANKS.

1. David Kirkpatrick. *The Facebook Effect: The Inside Story of the Company that Is Connecting the World*. New York: Simon & Schuster, 2010. Print. 33.

CHAPTER 2. TECH GENIUS IN THE MAKING

1. Jose Antonio Vargas. "The Face of Facebook: Mark Zuckerberg Opens up to The New Yorker." *The New Yorker*. Condé Nast, 20 Sept. 2010. Web. 15 Dec. 2011.

2. Ellen McGirt. "How Chris Hughes Helped Launch Facebook and the Barack Obama Campaign." *Fast Company*. Fast Company, 1 Apr. 2009. Web. 7 March 2012.

3. "Geek." *Merriam-Webster.com*. Merriam-Webster, 2011. Web. 7 March 2012.

4. "Nerd." *Merriam-Webster.com*. Merriam-Webster, 2011. Web. 7 March 2012.

5. Ann Hoevel. "Are You a Nerd or a Geek?" *CNN Living*. CNN, 2 Dec. 2010. Web. 7 March 2012.

6. David Kirkpatrick. *The Facebook Effect: The Inside Story of the Company that Is Connecting the World*. New York: Simon & Schuster, 2010. Print. 20.

7. Ibid. 24.

8. Ibid. 22.

9. Ibid. 26.

CHAPTER 3. THINKING BUSINESS

1. David Kirkpatrick. *The Facebook Effect: The Inside Story of the Company that Is Connecting the World*. New York: Simon & Schuster, 2010. Print. 30.

2. Ibid. 33.

3. Ibid. 134.

4. Ibid. 58.

CHAPTER 4. CALIFORNIA DREAMIN'

1. David Kirkpatrick. *The Facebook Effect: The Inside Story of the Company that Is Connecting the World*. New York: Simon & Schuster, 2010. Print. 44.

2. Ibid. 52.

3. Ibid.

CHAPTER 5. THIS IS SERIOUS BUSINESS

1. Oliver Chiang. "Mark Zuckerberg's Take On The Facebook Movie." *Forbes, 22 July 2010.* Web. 15 Dec. 2011.

2. Eduardo Saverin. "Facebook Co-Founder Speaks Publicly: What I Learned From Watching 'The Social Network.'" *CNBC.* CNBC News, 15 Oct. 2010. Web. 7 March 2012.

CHAPTER 6. BIG INVESTMENT

1. John Cloud. "The YouTube Gurus." *Time*, 25 Dec. 2006. Web. 7 March 2012.

2. David Kirkpatrick. *The Facebook Effect: The Inside Story of the Company that Is Connecting the World*. New York: Simon & Schuster, 2010. Print. 148.

CHAPTER 7. NEW DIRECTIONS FOR A NEW COMPANY

1. David Kirkpatrick. *The Facebook Effect: The Inside Story of the Company that Is Connecting the World*. New York: Simon & Schuster, 2010. Print. 143.

2. "Social Networking's Good and Bad Impact on Kids." *American Psychological Association.* American Psychological Association, 6 Aug. 2011. Web. 25 Dec. 2011.

3. Ruchi Sanghvi. "Facebook Gets a Facelift." *Facebook Blog.* Facebook, 5 Sept. 2006. Web. 16 May 2012.

4. David Kirkpatrick. *The Facebook Effect: The Inside Story of the Company that Is Connecting the World*. New York: Simon & Schuster, 2010. Print. 190.

SOURCE NOTES CONTINUED

CHAPTER 8. LOOKING AT REVENUE

1. David Kirkpatrick. *The Facebook Effect: The Inside Story of the Company that Is Connecting the World.* New York: Simon & Schuster, 2010. Print. 222.

2. Ibid. 224.

3. Ibid. 247-248.

4. Ibid. 248.

5. Ken Auletta. "A Woman's Place: Can Sheryl Sandberg upend Silicon Valley's male-dominated culture?" *The New Yorker.* Condé Nast, 11 July 2011. Web. 15 Dec. 2011.

CHAPTER 9. FACEBOOK, A GLOBAL PHENOMENON

1. Daniel Chai. "New Groups: Stay Closer to Groups of People in Your Life." *Facebook Blog.* Facebook, 6 Oct. 2010. Web. 7 March 2012.

2. Sam Biddle. "Facebook Just Killed Places." *Gizmodo.* Gizmodo, *23 Aug. 2011. Web.* 7 March 2012.

3. John Tenanes. "Our New Menlo Park Home." *Facebook Blog.* Facebook, 19 Dec. 2011. Web. 7 March 2012.

4. Sarah Kessler. "Zuckerberg to Potential Shareholders: Facebook Is on a Social Mission." *Mashable.* Mashable, 1 Feb. 2012. Web. 7 March 2012.

5. Damon Poeter. "Facebook IPO: Why Don't We Do It in the Roadshow?" *PCMag.* PC Magazine, 9 May 2012. Web. 22 May 2012.

6. Chunka Mui. "The Facebook IPO Is a Bust, Facebook Is Not." *Forbes.* Forbes, 22 May 2012. Web. 22 May 2012.

7. Farhard Manjoo. *The Great Tech War of 2012.* New York: Fast Company, November 2011. Print. 112.

INDEX

INDEX CONTINUED

ABOUT THE AUTHOR

Ashley Harris lives in Chicago, Illinois, where she works as Director of Corporate Relations at a leading design graduate school. She has authored several books for adolescents, including *Tupac Shakur: Multi-Platinum Rapper*, *Arms Trade* and for the *Essential Health: Strong, Beautiful Girls* series. Her work has appeared in *Time Out Chicago* and *Venuszine*. She holds a Master's degree from the University of Chicago.

PHOTO CREDITS

Paul Sakuma/AP Images, cover, 9, 65, 73, 79, 91; Craig Ruttle/ AP Images, 6; Markham Johnson/Polaris, 13, 14; Bill Greene/The Boston Globe/Getty Images, 17; Rick Friedman/Polaris, 25; Jason Kempin/Getty Images, 26, 97 (top); Press Association/AP Images, 28; Justine Hunt/The Boston Globe/Getty Images, 30; Juana Arias/ The Washington Post/Getty Images, 37; Los Angeles Times/Polaris, 38; Gonzalo Fuentes/Reuters, 43; Günay Mutlu/iStockphoto, 47; Charles Krupa/AP Images, 48, 96; Tony Avelar/AP Images, 52; GDA/AP Images, 55; Nati Harnik/AP Images, 56; Steve Jennings/ Getty Images, 62 ; Ahmad Faizal Yahya/Shutterstock Images, 66, 97 (bottom); Daniel Acker/Bloomberg/Getty Images, 70, 99 (top); Noah Berger/Polaris, 74; Keystone, Laurent Gillieron/AP Images, 82, 98; Ryan Anson/Bloomberg/Getty Images, 87, 99 (bottom); Tony Avelar/AP Images, 88; Jason Doiy/iStockphoto, 95